A TEACHING THEME
ON
CLASSROOM AUCTIONS

A TEACHING THEME

ON

CLASSROOM AUCTIONS

ASSERTIVE DISCIPLINE
IN
ACTION

RAYMOND "C" TIDD

November 2, 2001

To order additional copies of this book, contact:
Xlibris Corporation
1-888-795-4274
www.Xlibris.com
Orders@Xlibris.com
31069

This book is dedicated to my loving wife, Debbie, and to our wonderful daughters, Kelly and Lindsay.

CONTENTS

Meet the Author

Raymond "C" Tidd has used Auctions in his self-contained classrooms for the last 20 years of his 36 years in public teaching. He has found the whole process not only educational for the students but a great and fun way to teach responsibility.

ASSERTIVE DISCIPLINE

Teachers need help! With each passing year children need more and more positive direction and guidance from their teachers.

It's the teachers who are presented with overwhelming problems and decisions concerning their every day events in the classroom. Therefore, we as teachers find it difficult, to say the least, to deal with the pressures presented to us as teachers, as well as handling the needs of all our students.

With these thoughts in mind I have discovered a method of assertive discipline which is very positive, effective and exciting for all involved.

IT IS CALLED THE CLASSROOM AUCTION!

Teachers still need to do everything they have been doing as far as presenting lessons, reviewing, testing, and recording all the results for the purposes of giving grades, assessing, student growth, and supplying data to the administration and parents as it is requested.

What the classroom auction gives is more opportunity for the teacher to concentrate on teaching rather than so much time disciplining students.

I've used a classroom auction for the last twenty years (in grades 2 through 6) and have tried to streamline it so it has its maximum benefits. The greatest advantage of classroom auctions is that it allows the teacher to solve most of the discipline problems right in the classroom very quickly with very little loss of teaching time. This is better than sending students to the office on a daily basis which is very time consuming and an appearance of a loss of authority of the teacher to handle the problem in the classroom. Occasionally it is still necessary to send someone to the office because of the severe nature of the occurrence.

SETTING UP THE CLASSROOM

Before school starts I make sure everything is ready to go. The following needs to be done.

On one bulletin board I place a white cloud about six feet long and three feet wide cut out of butcher paper. The bottom of the cloud should be reachable by the shortest student in your class.

Next go to your local teacher store and buy thirty to forty yellow stars. Write the first name of each student in your class on the individual stars and place them on the cloud with a push pin. The names should be showing clearly and the push pin should be easy to push in and pull out.

While at the teacher store you can get 15 to 20 other cardboard figures or shapes either the same or all different.

Number these shapes with a black marker one through ten and also use numbers -1 to -5. Place the positive numbers one through ten to the right of the cloud evenly spaced throughout 2 or 3 walls of the room. These should be placed again so that your shortest student can reach them. The negative numbers are placed to the left of the cloud in order with the -1 first from the cloud and ending with -5. The negative numbers should also be reachable by your shortest students.

MONEY

All students love money and it does have value even though you print the money. The money is used by the students to buy certain things in the classroom and for those who learn how to save some of their money they can bid for items in your classroom auctions. The handling of money also teaches students responsibility in the care of the money they have earned.

I make a generic master and run off about 20 sheets. I like to get 10 bills (coins) on each sheet. See below the pattern used for the generic sheet with room for 10 bills (coins): (see page 21)

Take one of your generic money sheets and write your name, the school year, and your room number on each of the bills for that one money sheet. This will be your main master for the school year you are presently in. Save the other generic masters for other years. Run off about 50 (fifty) masters of this new master with your name, the school year and your room number on it. You now have 50 (fifty) sheets with the following on it:

Mr. Tidd Room 24

01-02

There should be 10 of these on each of the 50 sheets.

Now take *one* of the 50 sheets and place your 1st amount of money on each of the ten bills (coins) on that sheet. I like to start with 1 cent so they can learn how to work with all amounts of money. Your new sheet will now have ten of the following on one sheet:

```
Mr. Tidd Room 24
ONE CENT
01-02
```

Now run off about 50 sheets with the one cent on colored ditto paper. Every time I run off a new amount I use a different color of ditto paper. It makes the money easier to distinguish and it's more fun for all involved.

Once in a while I just can't get to colored paper and use white paper. But I go back to different colored paper on the next amount of money. Take the 50 sheets of the 1 cent money and cut them up with a paper cutter about 2" by

4" size. Don't let students use the paper cutter. They are very dangerous. You now have (10 x 50) or 500 1 cent coins stacked in neat piles for your use.

Generic Master

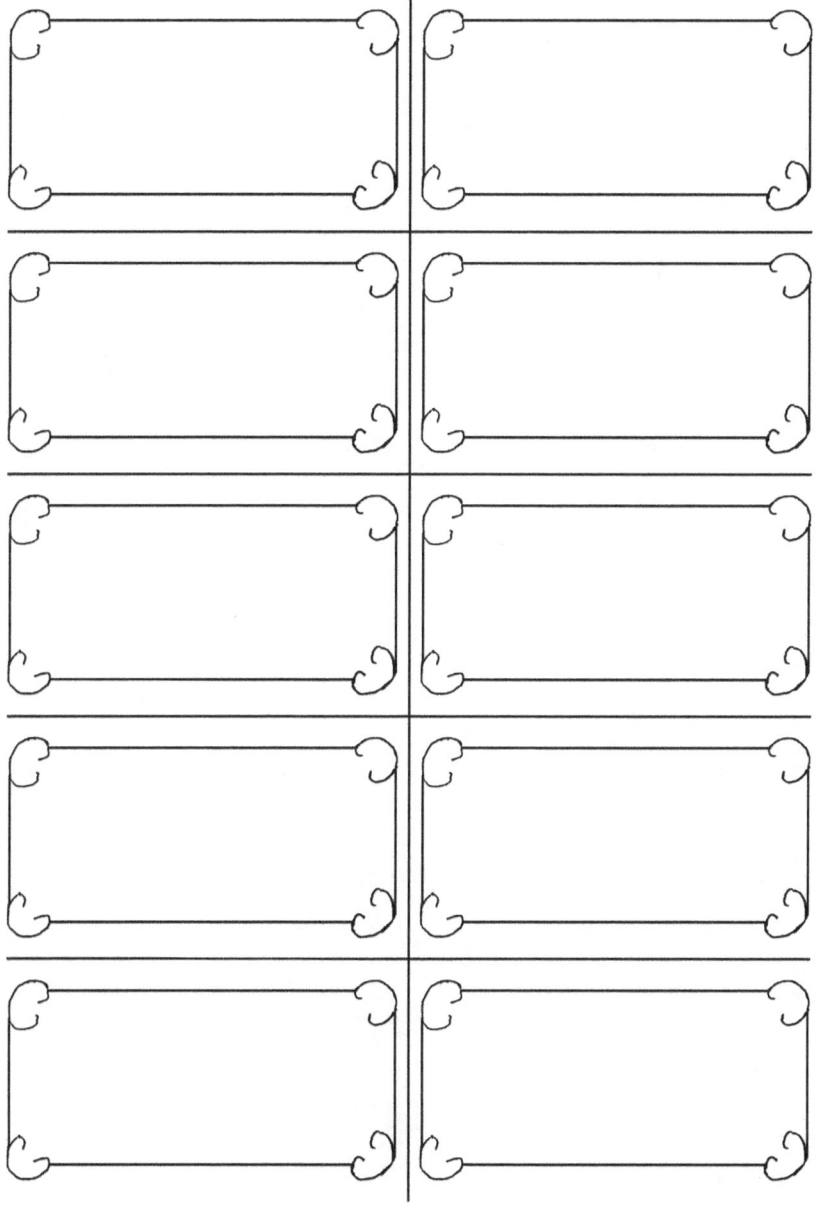

THE COST OF LIVING

Write up on the board in the front of the class the words

THE COST OF LIVING =

The cost of living equals what ever you want it to be. I start out with 1 cent and put it on the board:

THE COST OF LIVING = 1 cent

That means it cost the student 1 cent for *a new pencil,* 1 cent for *a drink of water*, or 1 cent for a *trip to the rest room.*

The first day of school I give every student in class 2 times the cost of living or 2 cents and then 2 times the cost of living for any new student thereafter, depending on what the cost of living is when the new student becomes a part of the class.

NOTE: As the cost of living goes up you will need from time to time to use another one of your 50 Masters and place on the new Master a higher amount of money as necessary for your convenience.

INFLATION

The first day of school I explain that supply and demand controls inflation so if we have a run on any item, e.g.: drinks of water, pencils or trips to the restroom, then inflation causes a hike in the cost of living. You as the teacher can raise the cost of living as you need to. I've raised it twice in one day or gone as long as two weeks without raising it. But any cost of living increase for one would then at be at the same time the same amount for all three, e.g.: drinks of water, pencils, or trips to the restrooms. One cost of living applies to all. It is important for students to realize that when I'm in the front of the room giving a lesson, they need to be at their desks, seated and listening. Therefore, any attempts to buy pencils or drinks usually cause a rise in the cost of living at that time. I allow a trip to the rest room without a rise in the cost of living. Here you need to use your best judgment and set up your own guidelines. I start the year with the cost of living being 1 cent. By the end of the year the cost of living is in the trillions. Students enjoy the new money values and it gives the teacher more control of the economy of supply and demand.

REWARDS

As students do good things throughout the school day I have them move up their stars one, five, or ten places on the wall. They place their star under the number and not on top of someone else's star. When students recall or answer difficult questions I sometimes have them move up their star 5 or 10 places depending on the difficulty of the question. If a student goes past the positive then on the bulletin board or your top positive number they can write their name on the front board and write next to it their new positive number, e.g.: *+15*. There are many reasons to move a star up and students like to move their star up. If they write their new number on the board then they need to return their star to the cloud. They can increase their number on the board if they make more points. If a student breaks *any* rule, they lose *all* their positive points and move their star to -1 through -5 depending on the infraction. Being the teacher you determine how serious the infraction is. It could be so bad they go to negative 10 or even negative 15. (your decision). If they do move their star down they lose *all* positive points. They also have to write 1 sentence for each move down telling what they did wrong. Example: If they were moved to negative 7 they would write 7 sentences. As soon as they write their sentences they can move their star back to *the cloud*.

EXPLORATORY TIME

At the end of the day (last 15 minutes approximately) (could be longer if the class deserves it), every student that has their work done can play chess, do art, or do research. Those students who still have work to do or who have to write sentences for being moved down do not have this earned time until they are done.

CLASS ELECTIONS

The first week of school the class elects class officers to help run the class. The President, Vice President, Secretary, and Treasurer and a couple more helpers of their choice pay the students the money they have coming. Say for instance Johnny's star was on 6, then he would get the cost of living times 6. If the cost of living is $1,000.00 then he gets 6 x $1,000 or $6,000.00. As soon as he is paid, his star goes back to the cloud. I allow the 1st 5 minutes of each school day for people to get paid and do any other odd jobs they may have to do. All students have at least one 5 minute job to do, like passing out papers, etc. I have new class elections every 7 weeks.

EXTRA WORK

On the board I always have extra credit math problems for students to work on in their spare time. Each student interested in trying one or more of the problems turns in each attempt to me during the day on a folded up paper and I put each attempt in my left pocket. The next day I tell them how they did and reward each student who did one or more of the problems right with the amount of money I was paying for that problem. They explain how they worked the problem out in front of the class. As the problems are worked out I replaced them with slightly harder problems. At the time we were doing the 6 extra problems below the cost of living was $1,000.00. All correct solutions were worth $200,000.00

6 EXTRA CREDIT

PROBLEMS

For One Day

VENN DIAGRAM

PROBLEM 4

The school cafeteria placed a special order for 110 Small cheese pizzas. Students were allowed to order one, two, or three additional toppings. When the pizzas arrived, there were:

25 with sausage, 45 with pepperoni, 48 with olives, 10 with sausage and olives, 8 with pepperoni and olives, 6 with sausage and pepperoni, 5 with all three toppings.

How many pizzas were ordered with no additional toppings?

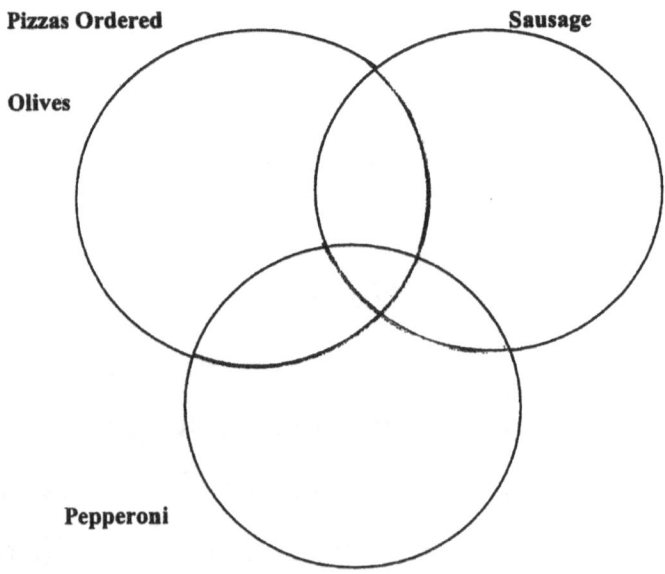

MAGIC SQUARE (SUM OF 52)

NAME _____

ALL 8 ROWS ADD UP TO "52"!

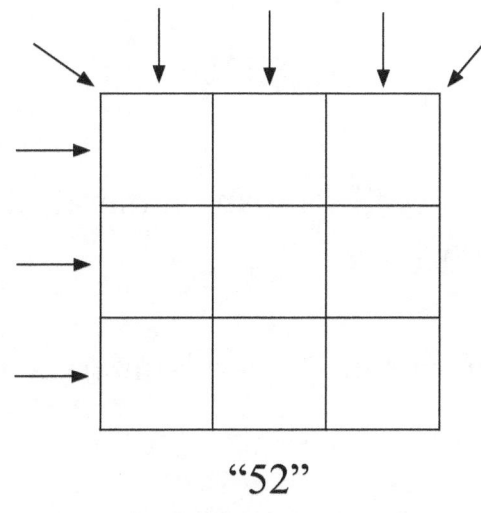

"52"

SUM LOOKING FOR

A new number (sum looking for) should be given each day. In order to increase students' learning, I make sure the 8 correct rows will require the use of some fractions from time to time.

Give (partial credit) cost of living amount for each row, which is correct. Can only use a number once. Give 100 times cost of living if they get all 8 rows correct.

605041 / 7 Long Division

Show All Work

XXXI Roman Numerals

(x) XXV
_____

Answer in Roman Numerals

ABCDEFGH How Many Different Pairs?

E.G.: AB, AC, AD, etc.

Write Down 21 coins that add up to $1.00

OTHER REWARDS

If the whole class is doing real well I write class on the board and put + 10 next to it. They get an extra 10 minutes at the end of the day for more exploratory time. If an adult gives them a compliment for good behavior they get a (+10). Some times when we are outside in line the class gets a compliment for being so straight (+10). When we walk to PE, Lunch, Library or Music, I ask them to keep arm's distance plus six inches. I also ask them to make right angles or 90° angles on the corners. They not only develop self-discipline, but they receive compliments and enjoy doing it at the same time while enjoying pride in themselves.

After recesses I move students stars up 1 move for each piece of trash they pick up on the playground. They show me their handful of trash and tell me the number of pieces they have picked up as they go into the classroom and put the trash in the trash can. I limit the number to 10 pieces and I trust them as to the number they tell me. Our class has received awards for keeping the school clean.

I also walk around the room and pay something for students reading during recreational reading.

I'm sure you can think of your own items you would pay for.

THE AUCTION

At the beginning of the year I write 100 on the board and tell the class I will subtract 5 from the number each day till we are down to 0 and then we will have our auction in two days. I also tell them that I will add 1 to the total for each piece of paper or trash I find on the floor over 1 inch long. Needless to say, we have a very neat floor.

When we get through the complete day and maintain our "0" on the board I announce to the class we will have our Auction in two days. The students are told to bring in the next day their small bills and exchange them for large bills so they can handle their money better. The next day we are exchanging money which teaches them something about adding and subtracting money. Class officers can help with this money exchange.

At this time I ask students to write down something they would like me to bring to the Auction. The class President takes the clip board around while they put down their name and what they want. I tell them if it is too expensive I will not get it (to keep it cheap!)

I also tell them they can bring something to the Auction too—but a person can only bring in one item. If one person brings in more than 1 item then I will put all that person's items into one pile and sell it altogether. (A package deal!)

That night I take the list and go shopping. Some might say teachers should not spend money on auctions but I feel it is a good investment in assuring a good classroom with a positive, happy environment. It's the best money you will ever spend. I buy a lot of colorful pencils, stickers, toy cars, cheap calculators, small stuffed animals, cheap chess set, etc. Very little over $5.00.

I try to get enough items so most students can get 3 items. Of course the students who saved the most money will do better in the bidding.

AUCTION DAY

I leave everything hidden till later in the day (usually in the car). I give every student a piece of paper and have them write their name and how much they lost in class or if something disappeared from their desk area. If they lost nothing, or in other words were able to keep track of their personal belongings and their play money, then they were to write nothing.

Then the President picks up the pieces of paper and gets together with the Vice President and Secretary and adds up how much the class lost as a whole. Next the President shows me the total and I write it on the board. It is now the classes responsibility to donate enough money to cover these losses. The President walks around the room with hat in hand. Before the President goes around I tell the class that if we cannot cover these losses as a class then I will have to pay for it out of the auction and they will have fewer items in the auction. It is truly amazing to see students donate to the cause of other students losses. After everyone is paid for their losses, we can get ready for the auction.

STARTING THE AUCTION

The teacher is the Auctioneer. I have laid everything out on a big table during recess or lunchtime. When they come in from lunch they gather around the table deciding what they each want. I have left the price tags on so they know how much things cost. Then I ask them to sit down and listen, and I give them the rules. NOTE! Students who need money during the auction can borrow from their friends.

First we must arrange ourselves into a semi-circle. Each student brings their own chair. (See Below)

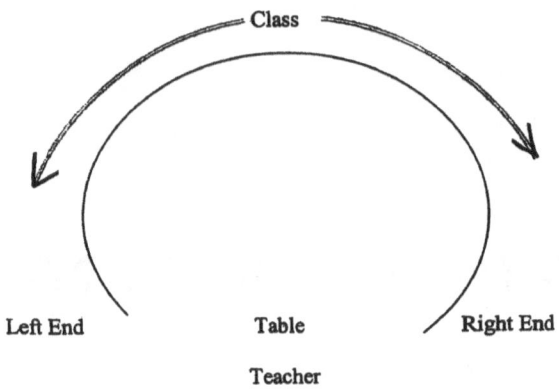

I mention that we must keep the noise level down or I will have to stop the Auction. I then flip a coin to see which end I will start with. The two on the end of the line can call the coin toss. If the left side wins the toss I will start over there and ask each person in order from left to right if they brought in something for the Auction. All students can bid on any of these items and buy any (or as many) of these items (as they want) according to the highest bidder. Use the going once . . . going twice . . . <u>Sold</u> (procedure)!

Note: Not all students will bring in something for the auction nor do they need to to be in the auction.

After I have gone through the whole class with items brought from home I then will start the auction with the items I brought in. Now a student can only buy one item for each of the 3 rounds.

Since I started on the left side before, now I start on the right side for the bidding for things I brought to the auction. It should be explained to all of the students that we must go through the complete class once with everyone getting one item each before we can bid on a second item in a second round. There will be a 3rd round for a 3rd item for each student only if there is enough time, and the students are well behaved.

Starting on the right side I ask that person to come up and pick an item from the table and make a bid on it. The bidding is now open to anyone else in the class on that item. Highest bidder gets the item. The next person in the row now picks an item. After a person buys an item in the 1st round he is not allowed to bid again in that 1st round but should sit quietly and watch.

After everyone has one item of things I bought at the store, then we start bidding for any second items left on the table. As soon as a student successfully bids for a second item and wins it, then they don't bid again till the next or 3rd and last round. After 3 rounds of store bought items the auction is declared over and any left over items go into the next Auction.

We now continue our count down on our 2nd 100 days and our next auction.

A FINAL WORD

Every class is different and every teacher has different ideas on rewards and consequences. It is this writer's hope that some ideas presented here can be of some help to every teacher's desire for a more orderly class using assertive discipline.

www.ingramcontent.com/pod-product-compliance
Lightning Source LLC
Chambersburg PA
CBHW061222280526
45784CB00006B/2598